# Nature Walks

**Supporting Learning in Schools**

the ods

ollinson

Hampshire
County Council

W

FRANKLIN WATTS
LONDON•SYDNEY

First published in 2010 by
Franklin Watts
338 Euston Road
London NW1 3BH

Franklin Watts Australia
Level 17/207 Kent Street
Sydney NSW 2000

Copyright © 2010 Franklin Watts

ISBN: 978 0 7496 9326 8

Dewey classification number: 577.3

A CIP catalogue for this book is available
from the British Library.

Planning and production by
Discovery Books Limited
Managing editor: Laura Durman
Editor: Clare Collinson
Picture research: Clare Collinson
Designer: Robert Walster, Big Blu Design

Photographs: FLPA: p. 14 (Steve Young),
p. 16 (Erica Olsen), p. 17 (Gary K Smith),
p. 18 (Paul Hobson), p. 19 (Imagebroker/
Winfried Schäfer), p. 20 (Nigel Cattlin),
p. 21 (Derek Middleton), p. 26t (Roger
Wilmshurst), p. 27t (Michael Hollings);
istockphoto.com: p. 6 (Vladimir Davydov),
p. 7 (Anatoli Dubkov), p. 12 (Jane McIlroy),
p. 24t (Claes Torstensson), p. 26b (Rick
Wylie); Shutterstock Images: title page
(originalpunkt), p. 8 main (vnlit), p. 8 inset
(Marcel Mooij), p. 9 (Dave Pilkington),
p. 10 (Rafal Olkis), p. 11 (Marie C Fields),
p. 13 (TRE Wheeler BA (Hons)), p. 15
(Gertjan Hooijer), p. 22 (fotosav), p. 23
(Alexander Chelmodeev), p. 24b (A
Jellema), p. 25t (Galyna Andrushko), p. 25b
(Sally Wallis), p. 27c (Mary Terriberry),
p. 27b (Emin Ozkan), p. 28t (Photoroller),
p. 28c (Planner), p. 28b (jamalludin).

Illustrations: istockphoto.com: pp. 7, 9, 14,
26bl (Hugo Lacasse), pp. 12t, 26br (joaquin
croxatto); Shutterstock Images: pp. 6, 26t
(Teodota Popovic), pp. 10, 22 (Shaber),
pp. 12b, 18, 27 (Nataly-Nete), p. 19
(Arcoindex), p. 20 (Sanderson Design).

Cover images: Shutterstock Images: main
(Jean Frooms), top left (originalpunkt),
bottom right (Kirsanov).

Printed in China

Franklin Watts is a division of Hachette
Children's Books, an Hachette UK company.
www.hachette.co.uk

## Nature walk safety

When you go for a nature walk
in the woods, go with an adult.

# Contents

Words that appear in **bold** in the text are explained in the glossary.

# Woodland wildlife

Let's go for a walk in the woods. A woodland **habitat** is a good place to discover many different plants and animals.

## UP CLOSE

As you walk along, look for wild flowers and other plants. Walk quietly and carefully, and listen for the sounds of wildlife.

Look, there's a squirrel on the branch of a tree.
It has found a nut to eat.

Let's see what other plants and
animals we can find.

# Woodland trees

What kinds of trees can we see in the woods?

**UP CLOSE**

Look out for acorns beneath oak trees – there may be animals nearby. Birds, squirrels and mice all love to eat acorns.

Here is an oak tree. Oak trees lose their leaves in the autumn and grow new leaves in spring. Trees that lose their leaves are called deciduous trees.

These pine trees are **conifers**, with spiky, narrow leaves called needles.

Most conifers are evergreen, which means they keep their leaves all year round.

# Fruits and seeds

What is the prickly thing growing
on this tree?

conker

fruit

It is a horse chestnut. Horse chestnuts are a type of **fruit**.
Inside the fruit is a **seed** called a conker. Look out for
conkers in the autumn, when the fruits fall to the ground.

Conifer trees have woody fruits called cones.
The seeds are inside the cones.

UP CLOSE

Fruits such as horse chestnuts have one large seed inside. Cones contain lots of seeds. How many kinds of fruits and cones can you find in the woods?

needles

cone

# Woodland plants

Trees are the biggest woodland plants.
What other kinds of plants can you find?

fern

ivy

moss

spurge

It is too shady in the woods for some
plants to survive, but mosses, ferns,
ivy and spurge grow well under trees.

Look, here is a carpet of bluebells!
Can you smell the flowers' sweet scent?

**UP CLOSE**

Like many woodland flowers, bluebells bloom in spring. The leaves on trees are young and so some sunlight shines through to the ground.

# Woodland birds

Woodland trees and other plants provide food and shelter for many different kinds of birds. This thrush has found some tasty berries.

**UP CLOSE**

As you walk along, listen for the sound of birds. Look high up in the trees, in bushes and on the ground. How many kinds can you spot?

Can you hear
a drilling
sound?

There is a
woodpecker
pecking a nesting
hole in a tree.
The hole will be
a safe place for the
woodpecker to lay its
eggs and raise its chicks.

15

# Woodland mammals

Many small **mammals** feed on woodland plants.
This little dormouse is searching for hazelnuts.

UP CLOSE

When the cold winter comes, dormice curl up in nests and sleep until spring. This is called hibernation.

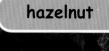
hazelnut

dormouse

antlers

sweet chestnut

UP CLOSE

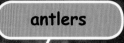

Male deer,
or stags, grow new
antlers every year.
During the **breeding
season**, they use their
antlers to attract
females and fight off
other males.

Woodlands are home to
some larger mammals, too.
Look, a deer has found some
nuts to eat. Deer also feed on
leaves and the bark of trees.

# A home in the woods

Woodland animals look for safe places to build their homes. Badgers dig deep underground tunnels in the soil. These are called setts.

**UP CLOSE**

It can be hard to spot badgers in the woods. They usually rest during the day in their setts and come out at night to feed.

Look, there is a fox coming out of its **den**.

Foxes often make their homes in old badger setts. Sometimes they even move in while the badgers are still at home!

# Woodland insects

Let's see what insects we can find in the woods.
Here is a tiger beetle running over some moss.

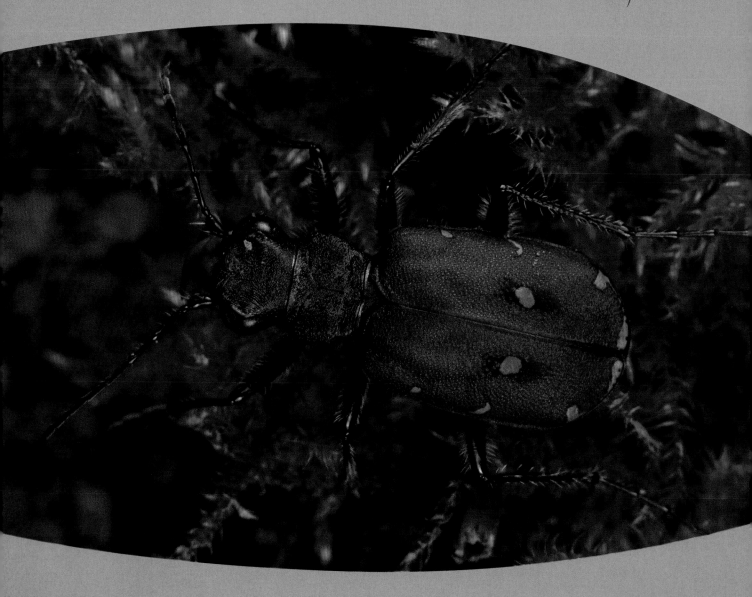

Insects hide in the **leaf litter**, on plants, among
fallen branches and on old tree stumps.

Some insects can be difficult to spot. Can you see a moth on this tree trunk?

UP CLOSE

Some moths use **camouflage** to help them hide from their enemies. Their colour and markings blend in with their surroundings so they are very hard to see.

21

# Fungi and lichen

Look at these bright red and white toadstools growing among the leaf litter.

UP CLOSE

If you see fungus growing in the woods, do not touch it or eat it. Fly agaric and some other kinds of fungi are very poisonous.

fly agaric

leaf litter

Fly agaric toadstools are a type of **fungus**.

What are these orange and green
patches on the trunk of this tree?

orange lichen

They are **lichens** growing on the bark. Lichens are
made up of fungus and tiny plants called **algae**.

# Through the year

A wood is a good place to look for wildlife all through the year. If you visit often, you will see how animals and plants **adapt** to the changing seasons.

## Spring

anemones

Spring is the season of new life. This is the best time to see white anemones, bluebells and many other kinds of woodland flowers.

## Summer

Summer is a good time to see wasps, bees and butterflies feeding on **nectar** in the woods. Look out for them on the flowers of blackberry bushes.

blackberry flower

# Autumn

In autumn, the leaves on many trees change colour and fall to the ground. Look out for cones, shiny brown conkers and other nuts in the leaf litter.

# Winter

In winter, many trees have no leaves. This is a good time to look at tree shapes and different kinds of bark. See if you can spot birds in the branches.

# Be a nature detective

When you go for a walk in the woods, be a nature detective and look for these things:

## Badger tracks

Look out for holes that might be entrances to a badger sett. Is there freshly dug earth around the holes? Are there badger tracks nearby?

## Squirrel's nest

If you see an untidy nest in a tree made of twigs or leaves, it may be a squirrel's nest, or drey. Look for holes in tree trunks, too. A squirrel may be nesting inside.

## Damaged bark

If you see bark missing from tree trunks, it may be a sign that deer are nearby. Deer often rub their antlers against trees and strip bark off the trunks.

## Fern spores

Ferns do not have flowers and they have **spores** instead of seeds. Look for the brown spores on the underside of fern fronds.

## Tree rings

If you see a newly cut tree stump, look carefully at the pattern of rings in the wood. A tree grows a new ring every year. Can you work out how old the tree was when it was cut down?

# Nature walk tips

As you walk through the woods, look all around and be as quiet as possible. Woodland animals will run to a safe hiding place if they hear you coming. Find a place to sit for a while, and see what you can spot.

Try not to disturb the wildlife you see. It is important not to touch eggs in nests or pick wild flowers. Do not touch fungus growing in the woods. It may be poisonous.

Take a notepad and pencil with you and make notes about the animals and plants you see or draw sketches of them. Then you can find out more about them at home or at school. You can look them up in books or on the internet.

If you have a camera, take it with you so you can photograph the animals and plants you see.

Binoculars will help you spot wildlife in the distance.

# Glossary

| | |
|---|---|
| adapt | to change to become more suited to a habitat |
| algae | tiny plants that do not have flowers, roots or leaves |
| breeding season | the time of year when animals produce young |
| camouflage | a way of hiding by blending in with the surroundings |
| conifer | a plant that makes cones |
| den | the home of an animal such as a fox |
| fruit | the part of a plant that contains its seeds |
| fungus | a living thing such as a mushroom or toadstool that grows on plants or rotting matter |
| habitat | the home of a group of animals and plants |
| leaf litter | a layer of rotting plant material on the ground |
| lichen | a small plant-like living thing made up of fungus and algae |
| mammal | an animal that feeds its young on milk |
| nectar | a sweet liquid produced by flowers |
| seed | the part of a plant from which a new plant can grow |
| spores | tiny parts of plants that can grow into new plants |

# Index